incorect poetry

An anthology of love, longing and loneliness

Volume IX

Copyright ©2019.
All rights
reserved.
Volume 9 of 12.

www.incorectpoetry.com
Ig @incorect_poetry
incorectpoetry@gmail.com

incorect poetry Volumes 1 - 12
Available on Amazon

Mistakes were made in life, love, spelling and grammar.

Disclaimer:

Due to a filing error on our part the physical copy paper stock is different. Volume I - VII are on glossy stock and Volumes VII - XII plain stock. If you are unsatisfied, please reach out at the above email address.

Thank you

I'll love you
Until
Tomorrow
Cause it's only a day away
I tell you I love you
I don't know what else to say
I say love
For lack of a better word
All I ask
Is for you to love me in return
For as long as you can
Or at least
Until you find
Your picture of perfection
For now
Stay with me
In my embrace
Holding hands
Loving in this moment
Forgetting about tomorrow

So allow me
To love you
For just today
Tomorrow isn't promised
Either of us
Might just go away
Then we'll never know
If this together
Would be forever
But what if forever
Was just for today
It'll feel like forever
As long as you stay

As I slowly drift
Into hopelessness
Of loves
Which will never be
No apologies
For the empty promises
Said so wholeheartedly
She kicks stones
Among the debris
In the places
Where there are parts of me

Here's to the moments
We missed
The love in this timeline
Doesn't exist
Due to a coincidence
When we should have kissed

If I only knew
I was loved
Felt like I was loved
Sometimes
I wonder
If it would help or hinder me
Would it blossom
Into something new
Or take away my creativity
Because this hurt is the ink
It all comes out whenever
I think of you

The men in line
For your love
Tend to remind you of
The lovers of your past
Like you're on repeat
They keep cycling through
Like it's a rollercoaster ride
They're there for the cheap thrills
Like you're an amusement park
Your body
A mere vessel
With a useless heart

I'm drunk right now
The closer I get to home
The more reckless I drive
Because I want to crash into your heart

If you ever fall in love
If you find the one
Prepare yourself
Prepare yourself for a broken heart
Because we all die alone
You'll realize it
When you're at their bed side
Holding their hand
Your heart crumbling
As they slowly slip away
Continue to live
Continue to love

Tired of drinking
This Kool-Aid
Of mixed emotions
Love
The most poisonous
Of elixirs

They say
Speak it into existence
I've written
So many poems
Made
So many declarations
And yet
Here I am

She's a pistol
I don't have a shot
At a woman of her caliber
She says chivalry is dead
Her heart turned to stone
I'm trying to be
The Arthur to her Excalibur

To the woman
I'd like to marry
I will never fully know you
Which is why
I'd like to spend everyday
With you
For the rest of our lives
To be there
With you
Experience
Every great and minor adventure
As we discover ourselves

To the bad habits of heart
To have known
You were trouble
From the very start
The vicious cycle
Of toxic lovers
To have infected you
Like all the others
The hole in my chest
From the amputation
Which still couldn't save me
From this terminal illness
We call love

As I gather the pieces
I hold them tightly
In an attempt to feel whole

To the hearts unforgiven
Which continue on living
On their own separate paths
The heart that used to be whole
Now two separate halves
To the end of forever
And the time wasted
To those nominal things
Like ducks and pickles
Which continue to remind you of her
While you still try to forget
To the oppressed emotions
The depressed commotions going on inside
Because you don't know
Whether it's love or hate

The simplicity
Of intimacy
Is ruined
By sex

If only

To be
At the other end
Of your lips

To the hearts
Used as skipping stones
To graze the lake of love
Only to eventually sink
Into the depths
Of loneliness
Lovelessness
Darkness

Standing by the shore side
Heartless

The dying art
Of Love
Chivalry
Already dead
Romance
Is on its last leg
No one wants to slow dance

The rubble
Now steppingstones
Of what was
Once a great wall

Now a gateway
To the most
Sacred of
Places. . .
My heart

The destiny of a fallen star
As you descend through the dark
Destination unknown
May you fulfill one wish
With your last
Fleeting breath

Between love and commitment

We remain distant
But at arms length
Because we can't
Just be friends
Love
Is more of an investment
Than either of us
Would care to make
Because we fear
The risk outweighs
The reward

We can phuck
Until our hormones content
But our hearts
Still hollow

To the scars
Of a healing heart
Are all
But a revealing part
Of the battles
You've endured
For the one
To call truly yours

Why is love
Such a Shakespearean play
Instead of a movie
We play
We play
We play
Then you see me
Act like you never knew me
Even though
I know
Our song
Still plays
In the beat of your heart

I'm afraid
Afraid
She'll see through
To the poverty
Of my heart
How broke
I really am
My riches
Have been stolen
Burglarized
By a pair of pretty eyes

Declarations of love
Screamed off the highest mountain
At the top of your lungs
Only mean as much as your presence

Go back to the one you love
Be there

She's a devil worshipping
Hell-raising woman
Her favorite position is
Six
Six
Six
She prefers men
With the mark of the beast
Heartless at least
Dark with the sharpest of teeth

Her chamber bellows
With the hollow screams
Of lost souls
Forgotten dreams
Broken promises
And empty wishes
Scorned by mankind
And all of men's loveless kisses

The art of your heart
You wish to be a masterpiece
But it's more of an
Obscure
Mangled
Abstract
Excerpt
From one of Picasso's forgotten dreams
To be a Warhol of colors
But your 3D glasses
Are in black-and-white
As much passion
As you push through your pen
You draw blanks
Haunted
By the silhouettes of desire
Scorned
By the faceless fire
Yet
You still yearn for its embrace
Because you see the sad girl
While everyone else
Is distracted Mona Lisa's smile

She craves
An out of body experience
To be torn out of her skin
Condemned for her sins
A sacrilegious self-sacrifice
A man
That will keep her up
Throughout the night
She likes them bad
Tires of these demons
In the pursuit of devils
Dreaming of the horrors of
Fallen rose petals

When you phuck me
It doesn't necessarily
Have to be all love
When you bite me
I expect it to be
With the intent
To draw blood
When you say my name
It better be
At the top of your lungs

www.ingramcontent.com/pod-product-compliance
Lightning Source LLC
Chambersburg PA
CBHW070803050426
42452CB00012B/2482